Dear Jack and Kate

This book is for you. I hope it
might show you that ordinary
things, which you pass every day,
can be so much more interesting
and entertaining and surprising
than you think.

If you look hard enough.

Other books by Bob Gill

Graphic Design Made Difficult 1992

Forget all the rules you ever learned about graphic design.
Including the ones in this book. 1981

Ups & Downs 1974

I Keep Changing 1971

Bob Gill's portfolio 1968

Parade
written with Keith Botsford 1967

The Green Eyed Mouse and the Blue Eyed Mouse 1966

Illustration: aspects and directions
written with John Lewis 1964

Graphic Design: visual comparisons
written with Alan Fletcher & Colin Forbes 1963

The Present
written with Alan Fletcher & Colin Forbes 1963

What Colour Is Your World? 1962

A to Z 1961

A Balloon for a Blunderbuss
written with Alastair Reid 1960

The Millionaires
written with Alastair Reid 1959

Unspecial Effects for Graphic Designers

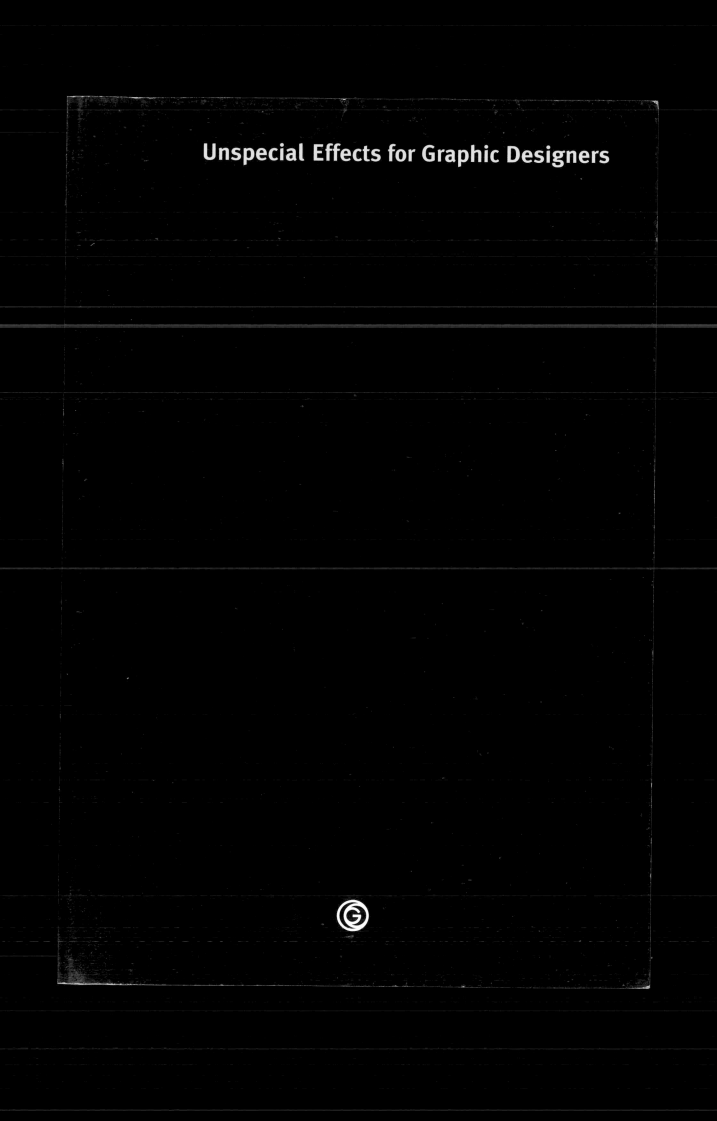

Contents

Previous page:
logo for a drinks
manufacturer.

And there's another thing about the situation today that designers must recognize.

Before computers, the production of printed matter was in the hands of designers and printers. Most clients had only the vaguest idea how it was produced. And they were prepared to pay well for their logos, newsletters, annual reports, brochures and other business paper.

But that's not the way it is now.

Now, for $99.99, it's possible to buy a program which allows anyone who can type and who has a computer and a scanner and a desktop printer to produce most of the stuff of the average business.

The mystique has finally gone out of ordinary design and print. These programs fit words and images into professional looking formats. They even throw in some *special effects*. And for low end commercial needs, that's fine.

So, if a typist can do much of the work previously done by well paid specialists, what's left for the designer? Designers have to do things that a typist with a computer *can't* do. This means that they have to be more ambitious, whether they like it or not.

Most designers, B.C. (before computers) were technicians with aesthetic pretensions. And, unfortunately, thinking is not the designer's first love. They love choosing colors, pushing type and shapes around, drawing in a particular style and imposing the latest graphic tricks on their next job, regardless of whether they are appropriate or not.

They get these tricks from the culture.

The culture has given them preconceptions about what's exciting, what's interesting; and most designers spend their time trying to emulate what's supposed to be hot, what's current, what's trendy.

But just think, if we want to do something the computer *can't* do, something that's original, how can we rely on what the culture tells us?

The culture tells all of us *the same thing*.

It's not Big Brother who's watching you, it's Disney and Time and Rupert Murdoch and a few other mega-corporations.

The culture which they inflict on us through their virtual monopoly of television, cable, film, theatre, magazines, CD's, etc., is designed to appeal to the lowest common denominator, which in turn, allows them to merchandise the greatest number of tchochkes: Bill and Hillary action figures, for example.

Of course, the establishment allows just enough high culture to prove that they're not Philistines.

How can you extricate yourself from this avalanche of white bread, so that you can be an original thinker?

The first thing is to purge your mind of as much cultural baggage as possible.

When you get a job, regardless of how familiar the subject, resist any temptation to think you know enough about it, and that you're ready to design. Assume that as all of the information and imagery was supplied by the culture mafia, none of the information or imagery is original with you.

Research the subject, as if you know nothing about it. And don't stop until you have something *interesting*, or even better, something *original* to say.

That's the most likely way of producing an original image.

Only when you're satisfied with the statement can the design process begin.

Try to forget what good design is *supposed* to look like. Listen to the statement. The statement will *tell* you what it should look like.

It will design itself. Well, almost.

Logo for *AGM,* a company which makes very small models.

My statement: regardless of how large the AGM, as on the side of a truck, it should always *seem* very small.

Problem:
TA, a logo for
*Television
Automation.*

My statement:
TA can also
say TV, at the
same time.

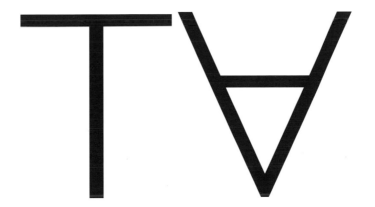

In thinking about a print logo for *Cooking TV*, a television show, I couldn't resist the first image that came to mind: a chef in a TV screen.

(I didn't follow my own theory of thinking of an interesting statement first, before thinking visually.)

However, I was reluctant to give it up. It communicated so well. *But it was boring!*

Cooking TV

Cropping the chef is better. It's stronger, but still boring *because the statement was boring.*

Cooking TV

Finally, an interesting statement: *the chef and her hat are too tall to fit inside the tv screen.*

Moral: sometimes, the dumbest, most obvious images can become original ones if pushed far enough.

Cooking TV

Logo for a
company which
rents guides.

Rent a New Yorker

My statement: Their guides are not out-of-work actors from Ohio, but *authentic* New Yorkers.

I gave the company a New York accent.

Renta Noo Yawka

A company
that gives
cast-off
computers to
schools and
charities had
a slogan
which was
interesting.

A computer is a terrible thing to waste.

It sounded like
a quotation.

"A computer is a terrible thing to waste."

So when I had
to use it as a
headline in an
ad, I thought
I might as well
go all the way.

"A computer is a terrible thing to waste."
William Shakespeare

Book jacket:
I began with a
maze which
was both
graphic and
difficult.

Graphic Design Made Difficult   Bob Gill

Then, I extended the maze to the back of the jacket. The back, when joined to the front, makes an image twice as wide.

And then, if another back was joined to the other side of the front, the image becomes three times as wide, and so on...

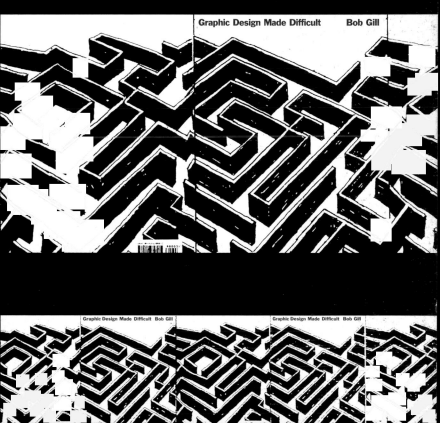

Graphic Design Made Difficult   Bob Gill

Graphic Design Made Difficult Bob Gill

Graphic Design Made Difficult Bob Gill

My wife and I
have separate
letterheads.

However,
there are
times when
a joint one
is useful.

I played with
the two sheets.

Bob Gill

Sara Fishko

One Fifth Avenue, New York, NY 10003   Tel: 212 460 0950

One Fifth Avenue, ...

Even I, with my very limited knowledge of science, know that everything in the universe is related in *some* way.

Therefore, no matter how *unrelated* two parts of a statement are, it should always be possible to incorporate both parts of the statement into a simple, single image. Less is more!

(On the other hand, more is more, too.)

Yabadoo Productions in association with Andrew C. McGibbon & Steven M. Levy present

Trophies

a new play by John Wooten

with **Janet Nell Catt, John Henry Cox, Mark Irish, Christen Tassin, Marc West**

Scenic Design: Mark Cheney. Lighting Design: Mark O'Connor. Costume Design: Missy West.
Stage Manager: Geoffrey F. Morris. Casting: Carol Hanzel & Elsie Stark.
Press Representative: Shirley Herz Associates. General Management: McGibbon & Levy Assoc.

Directed by **John Gulley**

Cherry Lane Theatre

38 Commerce Street (off 7th Avenue)
Box Office: (212) 989-2285
Tues.-Fri 8; Sat 3 & 8; Sun 3 & 7

A book jacket
with an image
of art directors
who give each
other awards,
and are bitter
rivals at the
same time.

Announcement:
a printer appoints
a consultant.

(The printer is
the one with
the dirty hands.)

**65th
Art
Directors
Annual**

The Kynock press is pleased
to announce the appointment of
Bob Gill as design consultant.

Logo for British
packaged goods
at international
trade fairs.

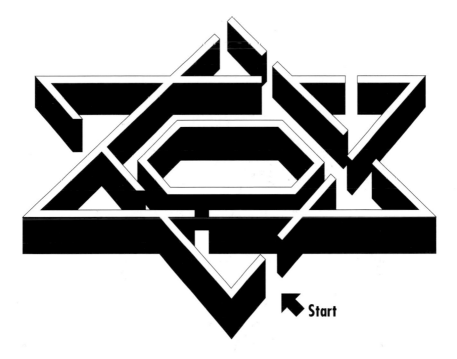

Logo for a
series of
radio programs
about what it
means to be
Jewlsh.

Start

Bob Gill's portfolio

Bob Gill's portfolio

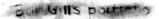

Dear Alan, Allegra, Amanda, Andrea, Ann, Anna, Barbara, Ben, Bernie, Bert, Bob, Bryce, Cal, Carol, Charlie, Charlotte, Cheryl, Dante, David, Dean, Deborah, Dorian, Ed, Elizabeth, Emily, Emma, Eric, Faith, Gary, Gene, Hadley, Ian, James, Jay, Jeremy, Jessica, Jill, John, Judy, Jules, Karen, Kate, Ken, Kendall, Kirk, Kristin, Larry, Laura, Lawrence, Leslie, Linda, Louise, Lucas, Lynn, Marcia, Marty, Mathew, Max, Milt, Nancy, Nick, Oliver, Otis, Pam, Paola, Rachel, Rebecca, Reggie, Robert, Rosie, Ruth, Sam, Sarah, Sharon, Simone, Steve, Susan, Suzy, Tim, Tracey, Vicki, and Zack.

Help us celebrate our Tenth Wedding Anniversary on Sunday, May 4th.
Please come and have a drink at apt. 8B, One Fifth Ave. any time from 3 to 6pm.
(No one will be admitted with a present.) RSVP please: 460-0950
Sara Fishko & Bob Gill

Letterforms can do so much more than spell words. They can communicate the *meaning* of the words, often as vividly as a picture can.

Sometimes, even more.

You'll laugh, scream, make new friends, get wet, have an adventure,
eat like a king, and be home by 8:30. Incredible Special Price of $84.95 includes:
Roundtrip Deluxe Coach, Free Raft Instruction & Guides, Safety Vests & Wet Suits,
Six Hour Raft Trip, Light Breakfast, Zabar's Gourmet Lunch.
Free Drinks on the Party Bus Going Home.
Tel: (212) 580-2828 for immediate registration.

Film logo:
illustrates
itself.

Logo:
a comedy
about a
character
who's in an
accident.

EVENING STANDARD
for small ads
ring FLE 3000

...ING STANDARD DAILY HOME FIND...

...OLD	SOLD	SOLD	SOLD	SOLD
...LD	SOLD	SOLD	SOLD	SOLD
...OLD	SOLD	SOLD	SOLD	SOLD
...LD	SOLD	SOLD	SOLD	SOLD
...LD	SOLD	SOLD	SOLD	SOLD
...OLD	SOLD	SOLD	SOLD	SOLD
...OLD	SOLD	SOLD	SOLD	SOLD
...OLD	SOLD	SOLD	SOLD	SOLD
...OLD	SOLD	SOLD	SOLD	SOLD
...LD	SOLD	SOLD	SOLD	SOLD
...LD	SOLD	SOLD	SOLD	SOLD

EVENING STANDARD
FLE 3000 small ads

CAFE FOR SALE Apply:	**SOLD**
FURNISHED **FLAT TO LET**	**LET**
VAN FOR SALE	**SOLD**
TYPIST WANTED	**FILLED**
Maisonnette	**LET**

He rang
FLE 3000
and
advertised
his car
in the
**EVENING
STANDARD**

SOLD

Television
sit-com logo
about a
secretary
who makes
lots of
mistakes.

It was created
on a thing
called a
typewriter.

Logo: an
architectural
draftsman.

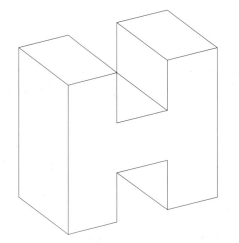

Illustration:
political magazine's
pessimistic
economic outlook.

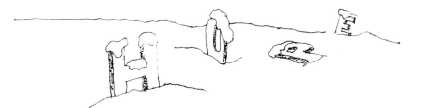

Avenue du Maine
Paris XIV
Telephone 326-4653

Logo:
*anti-apartheid
newspaper.*

Logo: *John Page,*
a sound recordist.

The price of
a magazine.

$Free

Logo: series of
informal
luncheons.

ᴸU.N.ᶜᴴ

Four ads
to persuade
designers to
submit work to
a competition.

Logo for
a play with
a French
title for an
English
speaking
audience.

I translated
it into
Yiddish.

(The schmuck)

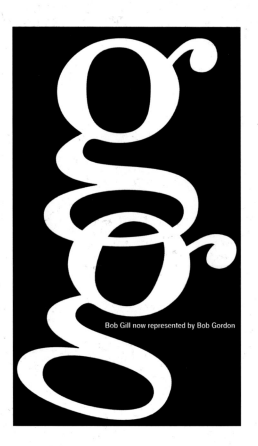

Bob Gill now represented by Bob Gordon

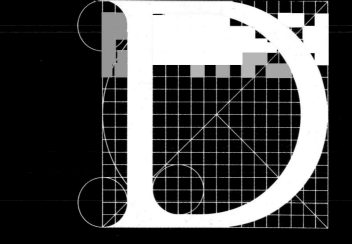

5. Interesting words/boring graphics

Take a statement like: we cure cancer for a nickel. It isn't necessary to make those words interesting. They *are* interesting.

If you try to make interesting words look interesting, the way they look competes with the words.

As there are trillions of images assaulting your audience, competing for their attention, the least you can do is not have the elements within your design (words and images) competing with each other.

Incidentally, the opposite is also true.

If you want to draw attention to an interesting image, the words that go with it shouldn't be unusual.

We
hate
small
print.

Invitation: *blackmails* the guests into bringing a bottle.

Dear Friends:

John Cole invites you to
a party on Sat. Sept. 9
at 8.30pm at 122 Regents
Park Rd. NW1 Flat D.
RSVP GRO 2291

Please bring a bottle.

Free Loaders:

John Cole invites you to
a party on Sat. Sept. 9
at 8.30pm at 122 Regents
Park Rd. NW1 Flat D.
RSVP GRO 2291

GOING TO SEE THE SOUTH AFRICAN 'WHITES ONLY' CRICKET TEAM?

(IT'S NOT CRICKET.)

Bob Gill, formerly blah, blah, blah and blah, blah, blah, blah, blah, blah, blah, blah, blah, blah. Founded blah, blah. blah, blah, blah, blah, blah, blah, blah, and blah. He recently blah, blah, blah, blah, blah, blah. blah, blah, blah, blah, blah, blah, blah, blah, blah. Awarded a blah, blah, blah, blah, and blah. blah, blah, blah, blah, blah, blah, blah, blah, blah. He then blah, blah, blah, blah, blah, blah. blah, blah, blah, blah, blah, blah, blah, blah, blah. blah, blah, blah, blah, blah, blah, blah, and blah blah, blah, blah, blah, blah, blah, blah, blah, blah. blah, blah, is now available for design, illustration and advertising projects at One Fifth Avenue, New York, NY 10003. Telephone: (212) 460-0950 Fax: (212) 460-8053 email: bobgilletc@aol.com

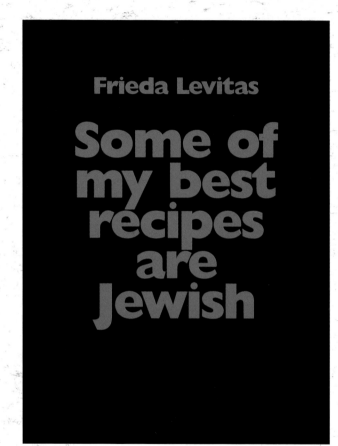

Frieda Levitas

Some of
my best
recipes
are
Jewish

Live theatre
is more exciting
than television,
movies or sports.

Well, maybe
not sports.

6. A few letterheads

Equinox Films, Inc.

200 West 72nd Street, New York, NY 10021
Tel: (212) 799-1515 Fax: (212) 799-1517
http://equinoxfilm.home.mindspring.com

Bob Gill.

GUEST CHECK

DATE	SERVER	TABLE NO.	NO. PERSONS	CHECK NO.
				468
			TAX	
		THANK YOU!		

One Fifth Avenue, New York, NY 10003   Tel. 212 460 0950
Fax: 212 460 8053   e-mail: BobGilletc@AOL.com

The very ordinary
scale in the lower
left hand corner
of almost every
map seemed a
fresh way to say
mapmakers.

CommunityCartography

0.05   0   0.05   0.1 miles

1 Lethbridge Plaza   www.ComCarto.com   a project of
Mahwah, NJ 07430   Fax: (201) 512-3825   Environmental Policy Services, LLC
1-877-MakeMaps   email: info@comcarto.com   and HydroQual, Inc.

Wylton Dickson Film Productions Limited

applied minds

655 north central ave.
glendale ca 91203
tel: 818 649 7900
fax: 818 649 8217
email: appliedminds.net

Carol Cutner
portrait photography
6 Radnor Lodge
Sussex Place
London W2
tel: 723 7645

The Creative Network
1849 Irving Street NW Washington DC 20010
Tel: 202 265 1522 Fax: 202 265 1243
e-mail: jperl@pop.dn.net

7. Odds and ends

Illustration: *left*.
op-ed piece about the
bald eagle becoming
extinct.

Children's book: *right*.
split-binding allows kids
to make words and
pictures from random
images and letters.

Illustration:
op-ed piece
about a
proposed
anti-terrorist
law that will
deprive
suspects of
their civil
rights.

Announcement that
Fletcher/Forbes/Gill
is one month old.

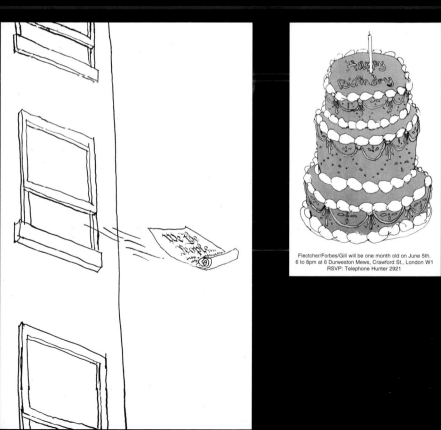

Flectcher/Forbes/Gill will be one month old on June 5th.
6 to 8pm at 6 Durweston Mews, Crawford St., London W1
RSVP: Telephone Hunter 2921

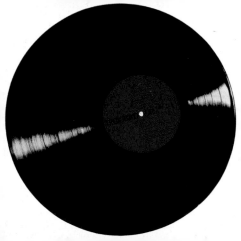

Logo:
lighting
designers.

Announcement of
the newest members of
the most exclusive
group of art directors
in the world, using
clip art and hack
typography, slapped
on the wall of a
derelict building.

May 9th is
's Day

Tie store logo:
a different tie on
every item of
stationery.

Illustration:
part of a folder
for a costume
rental
company.

I used the package of work that Fletcher/Forbes/Gill sent to Switzerland to be featured in the magazine, as the cover.

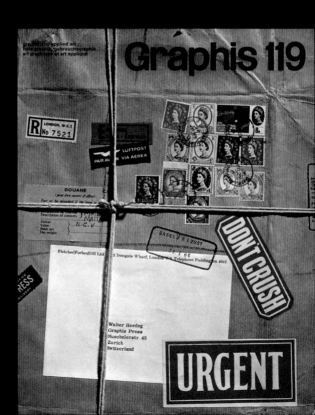

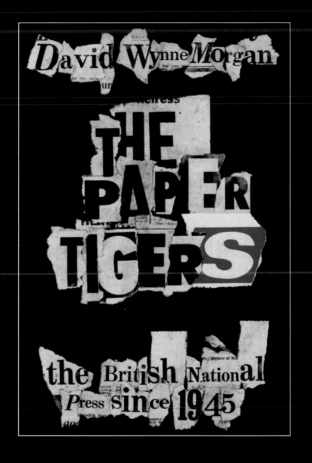

The Forum Gallery is moving to
745 Fifth Ave., New York, NY 10151 Tel: 212 355-4545   Fax: 212 355-4547
on December 1, 1991.

The twelve great Italian virtuosi known as I Musici will return to America in 1958-59. On previous visits, they established themselves unforgettably as the very reincarnation of the perfection, elegance and exuberance that were the glory of 17th & 18th century Italy.

Logo: a musical about a loser with big ideas.

A NEW MUSICAL

BIG DEAL

GOLDEN THEATRE
252 W. 45TH STREET

345

Presented to: Date of Issue: Authorized by

This Certificate for $25 will be honored at any Great American BackRub Store. Good toward the purchase of a BackRub or FootRub. Valid for six months. Not to be combined with any other Gift Certificate. Not redeemable for cash.

Package of radio
programs of two
comedians: one thin
and one fat.

Logo: *vintage
radio program
distributor.*

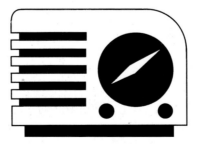

Sorry,

this may be your last chance to receive
The Learning Annex. Costs are too high to continue
mailing...unless you register for a class now!

Slipper
display.

Leaflet.

2 Men's Shetland
Sweaters for $59.

Bancroft Since 1947
863 Madaison Ave., 477 Madison Ave., 54 W.50th St., 575 Lexington Ave.
1250 Avenue of the Americas, 45 West 48th Street.

Advertising's best friend

In addition to TV Guide's vitality, opinionated writing, and glamorous photos, our strength also lies in its local capabilities. 1998 will see more multiple covers for special issues, such as the 30+ team covers for theNFL Preview issue and the regional baseball and NASCAR covers.So whether your target is women with a passion for fashion, men who love sports or parents looking for direction, TV Guide delivers nearly 40 million readers.

Booklet cover:
magazine
readership
survey.

Newspaper ad:
a musical about
the choreography
of Bob Fosse.

"The Learning Annex? We don't read it."

"Trust me. I'm going
to win an Emmy,
an Oscar, and a Tony,
all in the same year,
and one day they'll
even do a musical
about me."

"Sure."

Logo: a ballet
which depicts
all men as
sadists, and all
women as
whores.

As the ballet
is about
stereotypes,
I made the
dancers into
cardboard
figures.

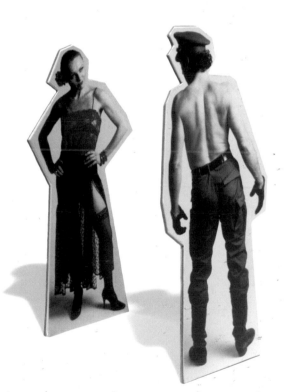

MAY 1981
$1.75

AMERICAN ARTIST®

ICD

Illustration:
one of a series
of images of
British graphic
design.

(No insult
intended.)

Logo:
a jazz musical.

From

to

Zev Bufman, Ken Butler, Walter Barnett and Ivan Bloch present (in alphabetical order)

JOHN LITHGOW GEORGE SEGAL

MARIA TUCCI
in The Long Wharf Theatre Production of

ROD SERLING'S REQUIEM FOR A HEAVYWEIGHT

John Lithgow, George Segal, Maria Tucci in Rod Serling's Requiem for a Heavyweight
with Cosmo F. Allegretti, John Capodice, Kevin Carrigan, Dominic Chianese, Joyce Ebert,
Daniel F. Keyes, John C. McGinley, John C. Moskoff, Herbert Rubens, Mike' Starr,
Eugene Troobnick, Ellis "Skeeter" Williams and

DAVID PROVAL

Sets: Marjorie Bradley Kellogg, Costumes: Bill Walker, Lighting: Ron Wallace
General Management: Theatre Now, Inc. Casting: Deborah Brown
Production Stage Manager: James Harker, Associate Producer: Jay M. Coggan
Produced in association with Japanese Theatres/Richard G. Wolff, President.
Originally presented by Long Wharf Theatre, New Haven, Connecticut.
Arvin Brown: Artistic Director, M. Edgar Rosenblum: Executive Director

Directed by

ARVIN BROWN

Martin Beck Theatre
302 W. 45th St.

A theatre's gift to
corporate donors: a
silk screen print of
playwrights.

Some of the company our company welcomed to Indiana since 1972.

Seated: L to R. T.S. Eliot, Somerset Maugham and Tennessee Williams. Standing: L to R: George Bernard Shaw, August Strindberg, Harold Pinter, Arthur Miller, Oscar Wilde, Charles Dickens, Neil Simon, Agatha Christie, Tom Stoppard, Anton Chekov, Thornton Wilder, William Shakespeare, Hendrik Ibsen, Lillian Hellman and Noel Coward.

Produced for the friends of the Indiana Repertory Theatre on the occasion of their Twentieth Anniversary.

1. Antonio Vivaldi
2. Gabriel Faure
3. Peter Ilyich Tchaikowsky
4. Jean-Philippe Rameau
5. Ferruccio Busoni
6. Edward Elgar
7. Sergei Rachmaninoff
8. Philip Glass
9. Giacomo Puccini
10. Maurice Ravel
11. Aaron Copland
12. Carl Czerney
13. Nicolai Rimsky Korsakov
14. Modest Mussorgsky
15. Alexander Scriabin
16. Sergei Prokofiev
17. Arnold Schoenberg
18. Giuseppe Verdi
19. Karlheinz Stockhausen
20. Jean Sibelius
21. Richar Strauss
22. Franz Liszt
23. Franz Schubert
24. Clara Wieck Schumann
25. George Frederic Handel
26. Richard Wagner
27. Johannes Brahms
28. Hector Berlioz
29. Christoph Willibald von Gluck
30. Carl Maria von Weber
31. Edvard Grieg
32. Virgil Thompson
33. George Gershwin
34. Johann Sebastian Bach
35. Frédéric Chopin
36. Heitor Villa-Lobos
37. Franz Joseph Haydn
38. Robert Schumann
39. Felix Mendelssohn
40. Paul Hindemith
41. Bedrich Smetetana
42. Claude Debussy
43. Cesar Franck
44. Gustav Mahler
45. Domenico Scarlati
46. Camille Saint Saens
47. Leonard Bernstein
48. Antonin Dvorak
49. Ludwig von Beethovan
50. John Cage
51. Wolfgang Amadeus Mozar
52. George Bizet
53. Igor Stravinsky
54. Ralph Vaughan Williams
55. Bela Bartok
56. Erik Satie

From
Campbell's Soup Company

to
The American Iron & Steel Institute

MG Productions
216 East 45th Street, New York, NY 10017-3374
Tel: (212) 682-4525 Fax: (212) 818-0627

Indiana
Repertory
Theatre

Logo:
a video production
company wanted to
position itself
as "cutting edge."

As "cutting
edge" imagery is
bound to date,
I went to the
other extreme.

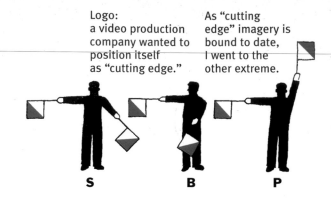

S   B   P

Logo:
an *entertainment
conglomerate*
wanted to project
an exciting image.

The *i* is for their
initial, and the *!*
is for their image.

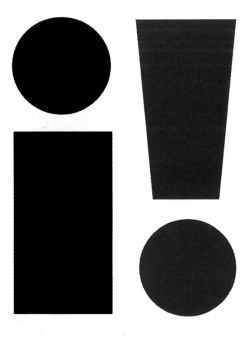

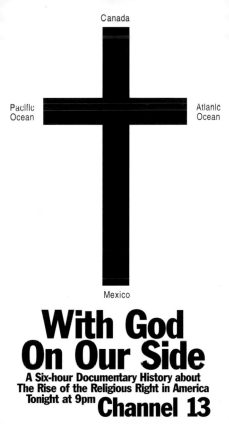

Canada

Pacific
Ocean

Atlanic
Ocean

Mexico

With God On Our Side

**A Six-hour Documentary History about
The Rise of the Religious Right in America
Tonight at 9pm** Channel 13

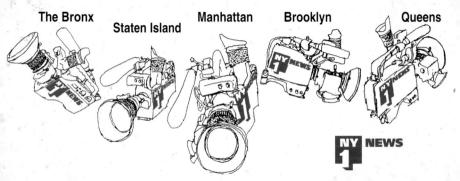

The Bronx · **Staten Island** · **Manhattan** · **Brooklyn** · **Queens**

EMI Film Productions Limited present

Julie Christie
Alan Bates
"The Go-Between"

directed by Joseph Losey
introducing Dominic Guard / screenplay by Harold Pinter
music by Michel LeGrand

executive producer Robert Velaise / produced by John Heyman & Norman Priggen
Official British Entry Cannes Film Festival 1971

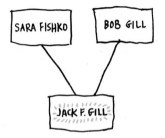

Sara Fishko and Bob Gill announce the arrival of their son, Jack
at 6:14am on October 28, 1988

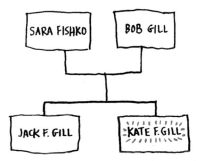

Sara Fishko and Bob Gill are pleased to announce the birth of
their daughter, Kate, November 21, 1991 at 11:31pm; 6 lbs. 12oz.

8. On the other hand...

Did I say, "forget special effects, stick to reality ?"

Fine, but occasionally, an exaggerated image reveals more about reality than a literal one.

Ecumenical
season's greetings
image.

Illustration in
an annual report
for a company
with offices in
New York and
London.

illustration:
*working at
home.*

Logo:
*2 one-act
plays.*

ROCK'N ROLL!
The first 5,000 years.

A multi-media musical event. Live.

St. James Theatre
246 West 44th Street, New York City 10036

Ads for a
film with an
ironic title.

Film logo:
Julius Caesar.

Booklet cover:
the information highway.

Illustration:
traffic.

Illustration:
smoking a pipe
gives people an
elegant persona.

Logo: a play
about a magician
involved in murder.

Eleven, in
a 365 page
calendar
for a charity,
in which each
designer did
one number.

Logo and poster:
plotless musical
featuring many
styles of dancing.

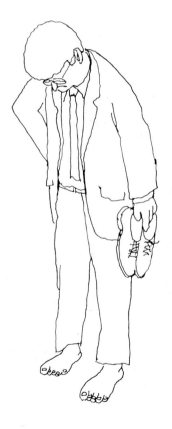

Illustration:
mechanical
energy.

This photogram
(remember
photograms?)
was made up
from various
watch parts.

Illustration:
indiscriminate
chewing up
of the green
belt for more
shopping malls
and theme
parks.

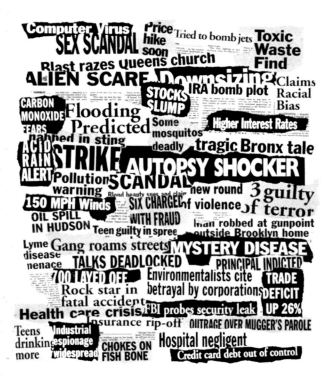

The Great American Backrub wishes you a stress free holiday.

Gene Wolsk presents Mastergate: a Play on words by Larry Gelbart
Scenery by Philipp Jung. Costumes by Candice Donnelly.
Lighting by Stephne Strawbridge. Video by Dennis Diamond.
Sound by Stephen Santomenna. Casting by Simon/Kumin, C.S.A.
Directed by Michael Engler.
                              Criterion Center: Broadway & 45th St.

Logo for a
musical with
two stars who
were promised
equal billing.

Logo:
film production
company with
two directors.

FUCCI   STONE

Magazine
cover:
(my first.)

If you can stand it, we can do it.

No middlemen. All of the work is done on our own premises.
Call the Decorator's Workroom at (212) 766-1655 and you'll see.

Illustration:
heated debate
between two
scientists.

The Mattei Affair
a film by Francesco Rosi   with Gian Maria Volonte
Gran Prix: Cannes Film Festival   Gate Cinema

Twelve designers
were each asked to
design one month
of a calendar for
a charity.

My theme: *growth*.

1976
September

Sun   Mon   Tues   Wed   Thurs   Fri   Sat

Illustration
in a booklet
promoting
a seminar
on the
Broadway
musical.

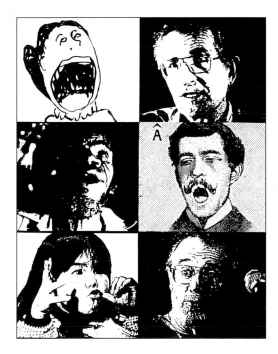

Film logo:
*The Human
Language.*

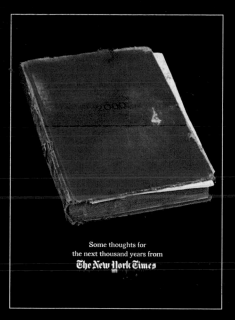

Some thoughts for
the next thousand years from
The New York Times

9. A paradoxical diary

There are infinite ways to upset people's visual equilibrium. I hope to try them all. I've always been fascinated by images that make sense at first, but turn out to be impossible, or images which although they are impossible, have their own internal logic.

I collected lots of interesting thoughts of some of the world's brilliant thinkers, and arranged them in pairs which contradicted each other.

I then illustrated the pairs with contradictory images.

"Some things have to be seen to be believed.
S. Harwood

Presidents' Day
Monday, February 21

Washington's Birthday
Tuesday, February 22

Wednesday, February 23

"Some things have to be believed to be seen."
Ralph Hodgson

Thursday, February 24 Friday, February 25 Saturday, February 26
                                Sunday, February 27

"Whom the gods wish to destroy they first make mad."
Euripides

Monday, March 20   Tuesday, March 21   Wednesday, March 22

"Whom the gods wish to destroy, they first call promising."
Cyril Connolly

Thursday, March 23 | Friday, March 24 | Saturday, March 25
Sunday, March 26

"Love thy neighbor as thyself."
Genesis xix:18

Monday, September 18 | Tuesday, September 19 | Wednesday, September 20

"Kindness is in our power, but foundness is not."
Euripides

Thursday, September 21   Friday, September 22   Saturday, March 25
Sunday, March 26

Why climb a mountain? "Because it is there."
George Mallory

Monday, December 4 | Tuesday, December 5 | Wednesday, December 6

Why do writers write? "Because it isn't there."
Thomas Berger

Thursday, December 7   Friday, December 8   Saturday, December 9
Sunday, December 10

10. 20/20 hindsight

One of the advantages of putting a book like
this together is the chance to take another
look at my old jobs.

I wish I could do some of them over.

On the next few pages are some very obvious
examples of how I failed to go as far as
possible with the solution.

Bob Gill no Brazil
Museu da Imagem e do Som
Av. Europa, 158 São Paulo

Exposição 22 janeiro a 17 fevereiro 1991

Bob Gill no Brazil Museu da Imagem e do Som
Av. Europa, 158 São Paulo
Exposição 22 janeiro a 17 fevereiro 1991

Bridges is a series
of radio programs
in which
conservatives
debate liberals.

The entangled
wires are supposed
to represent the
conflicts of the two
positions.

The wires
should have
been even *more*
entangled.

Forget all the rules about graphic design. Including the ones in this book.

By Bob Gill.

The body is from Caesarea, the head is from Putney.

The body is Roman, 2nd or 3rd Century - not a good year for statues. The head is Anglo-Saxon, 1963 contemporary. She got to Israel by El Al Boeing in four and a half hours. There are two-week holidays from 95 gns - including hotel and jet flight. Write for information to The Israel Government Tourist Office 59 St. James St., SW1

Bob Gill: "Coping with the Philistines."

A public lecture and slideshow for designers, art directors, and their clients. Thursday, March 1, 1990 at 8pm in the Alberta College of Art lecture hall. Tickets: $10. Students: $8.

Design and advertising problem solving workshop for professionals: Friday and Saturday, March 9 and 10, 9am to 5pm. Fee: $265. Workshop limited to 25 participants only.

For information/registration, contact △ The Alberta College of Art Extension Department, 1407 14th Ave. N.W., Calgary, Alberta, T2N 4R3. Telephone: (403) 284-7640

Bob Gill is a designer, an illustrator, a copywriter, and a teacher.

After freelancing in New York, he went to London on a whim in 1960 and stayed 15 years. He started Fletcher/Forbes/Gill, a design office with the two brightest designers in England.

F/F/G began with two assistants and a secretary. Today, it's called *Pentagram,* with offices everywhere except Tibet.

Gill resigned in 1967 to work independently in London.

He returned to New York in 1975 to write and design *Beatlemania,* the largest multi-media musical up to that time on Broadway, with Robert Rabinowitz, the painter.

Gill still works independently and still teaches. He's had one-man shows in Europe, South America, the Far East and in the US.

He was elected to the New York Art Directors Club Hall of Fame in 1991 and the Designers and Art Directors Association of London recently presented him with their Lifetime Achievement Award.

He's now living in New York with his wife, New York Public Radio's Sara Fishko, their son, Jack, and their daughter, Kate.

Client/Publisher	Description	Colaborators	Date	Page
AGM	Logo	Photo: J. Summerhayes	1968	13
Alberta School of Art	Poster	Photo: M. Jacobs	1990	154
American Artist Magazine	Cover		1981	92
Anthony Blond Ltd.	Book Jacket: *Paper Tigers*		1973	79
Anti Apartheid Movement	Poster: *Cricket*		1964	54
Anti Apartheid Movement	Newspaper masthead		1964	44
Applied Minds	Letterhead		2000	64
Art Direction Magazine	Cover		1957	127
Tina Ball	*Two plays*		2000	111
Bancroft	Leaflet: sweaters		1994	88
Bancroft	Mother's Day poster		1994	75
Steve Baum	*Computer*		1998	20/21
Steve Baum	Logo		1999	102
Charles Black Publishers	*I Keep Changing*		1975	160
Broadway seminar	Folder		1995	135
Zef Buffman	Poster: *Requiem...*	Photo: M. Jacobs	1990	96
CBS Television	Title: Private Secretary		1954	41
John Cole	Invitation		1977	53
Columbia Pictures	Logo: *Casey's Shadow*		1983	39
Columbia Pictures*	Ads: *...and justice for all*	Photo: M. Jacobs	1981	113
CommunityCartography	Letterhead		2000	62
Concert Associates	Program cover: *I Musici*		1959	82
Cooking TV	Logo	Photo: M. Jacobs	1997	16/17
Creative Network	Letterhead		2000	65
Carol Cudner	Letterhead	Photo: J.Summerhayes	1971	65
Cystic Fibrosis Foundation	Concert program cover		1983	95
D&AD	Ad campaign		1970	46
Datascope	Logo		1995	49
Decorator's Workroom	Newspaper ad		1998	131
Wilton Dickson	Letterhead	Photo: J.Summerhayes	1974	63
El Al Israel Airlines	Ad	A. Fletcher/C. Forbes	1965	154
EMI Films	Poster: *The Go Between*	Photo: unknown	1973	105
Equinox Films	Logo: *Human Language*	Photos: various	1997	135
Equinox Films	Letterhead		1999	60
Evening Standard	Poster campaign	A. Fletcher/C. Forbes	1964	40
Jules Fisher	Logo: *Big Deal*	Photo: M. Jacobs	1986	83
Jules Fisher	Logo and poster: *Dancin'*	Photo: J. Mitchell	1980	120
Jules Fisher	Logo: *Dangerous Games*	Photo: M. Jacobs	1987	91
Jules Fisher	Logo: *Now You See It*		1994	118
Jules Fisher	Poster: *Rock 'n Roll...*	Photo: M. Jacobs	1985	112
Jules Fisher	Poster: *The Rink*	Photo: M. Jacobs	1986	128
Fishko/Gill	Birth announcements		88/91	106/107
Fishko/Gill	Invitation		1997	35
Fishko/Gill	Letterhead		1997	24/25
Fletcher/Forbes/Gill	Announcement	A. Fletcher/C. Forbes	1960	69
Fortune Magazine	Earth mover		1961	123
Fortune Magazine	Mechanical energy		1959	122
Fortune Magazine	Traffic		1958	115
Forum Gallery	Moving announcement	Photo: S. Parik	1990	81
Fucci/Stone	Logo		1995	130

Client/Publisher	Description	Collaborators	Date	Page
Gate Cinema	*Mattei Affair*		1970	133
Geers/Gross Advertising	Telephone booths		1994	110
Bob Gill	Announcement: *Blah, blah...*		1976	55
Bob Gill	Booklet cover: *Logos*		1999	84
Bob Gill	Invoice		2000	61
Bob Gill	Season's greetings		'98/'00	74/110
Bob Gordon	Announcement		1957	48
Graphis Magazine	Cover	A. Fletcher/C. Forbes	1969	78
Graphis Magazine	Logo: *Them/Us* conference		2000	119
Great American Backrub	Gift certificate		1997	85
Great American Backrub	Season's greetings		1996	124
Grey Advertising*	Poster: *La Bete*		1998	47/93
Brian Harvey	Logo	Lettering: George Hoy	1969	42
Victor Herbert	55		1977	43
High Times Magazine	Illustration: scientists		1988	132/133
Indiana Rep. Theatre	Cover: fund raising booklet		1989	101
Indiana Rep. Theatre	Cover: live theatre booklet		1989	57
Indiana Rep. Theatre	Illustration: playwrights		1989	129
Insight Corporation	Logo		2000	102
Interiors	Magazine cover		1952	130
Elliott Kastner	Film logo: *Julius Caesar*	Photo: J. Summerhayes	1977	113
Kynock Press	Announcement		1975	31
The Lawyer Magazine	Cover		1969	30
The Learning Annex	Ad: white water trip		1988	38
The Learning Annex	Magazine insert		1990	87
The Learning Annex	Illustration: *working at home*		1990	111
The Learning Annex	Poster: *No calories*		1991	125
The Learning Annex	*$Free*		1988	44
The Learning Annex	*Readership survey*	Photo: M. Jacobs	1989	90
Little, Brown	*A to Z*		1962	68
Livent*	Ad: *Fosse*	Photo: unknown	1999	90
Lumiere Productions	Ad: *Religious Right*		1997	103
Lund Humpries	Book jacket: *Gill's portfolio*		1970	34
Martins Rent-a-car	Cover: *We hate small print*		1974	52
Elizabeth McCann	Poster: *Total Abandon*		1974	28
MG productions	Trade ad: *soup to nuts*		1989	100
Museu da Imagen	Poster: Gill exhibition		1965	148/149
Name withheld*	Illustration: *first soft drink*		1991	129
Name withheld*	Logo: *various drinks*		1993	5
Nappi/Eliran Advertising	Logo: *High Rollers*		1994	94
The Nation	Illustration: *hope*		1997	42
New York AD Club	Book Jacket	Photo: M. Jacobs	1986	31
New York AD Club	Poster: *Hall of Fame*	Photo: C. Fischer	1988	72/73
New York One Television	Bus side poster		1994	104
The New York Times	Diary		1998	137-145
The New York Times	Illustration: *constitution*		2000	69
The New York Times	Illustration: *eagle*		1997	68
Robert Norton	Calendar		1975	134
Nova Magazine	Illustration: *pipe smoker*		1968	116/117

Client/Publisher	Description	Collaborators	Date	Page
Observer Magazine	Illustration: *British design*		1999	93
ORT	Jacket: *Cookbook*		2000	56
John Page Sound	Logo	A. Fletcher/C.Forbes	1980	44
Pirelli slippers	Point of sale display		1967	88
Queen Magazine	Illustration: *Jazz*		1960	114
Queen Magazine	Illustration: *Montgomery, AL.*		1960	97
Queen Magazine	Illustration: *Two left feet*		1974	121
Radio Foundation	Package: *Bob & Ray*		1999	86
Radio Foundation	Logo		2000	86
Radio Foundation	Logo: *Bridges*		2000	150/151
Radio Foundation*	Logo: *What is a Jew?*		2000	33
Renta Noo Yawka	Logo		1999	18/19
RLF Corp.	Eleven		1997	118
Joel Schenker	Logo: *Horowitz*		1992	39
School of Visual Arts	Moving poster	Photo: R. Rojas	1956	80
Robert Scott	Illustration: straw hat		1958	77
Television Automation	Logo		1980	14/15
Third Eye	Logo		2000	71
The Tie Store*	Logos		2000	76/77
The Troubadour	Record cover: Colin Bates	Retouching: W. Sporel	1967	70
Town Magazine	Illustration: old age home		1970	75
TV Guide*	Trade ad		1991	89
U.K. Board of Trade	Logo: packaged goods	Lettering: George Hoy	1969	32
U.N. Association	Logo: *luncheon*		1971	45
Van Nostrand Reinhold	Book jacket: *Forget rules...*	Photo: M. Jacobs	1981	152/153
Watson-Guptill	Book Jacket: *Graphic Design...*		1988	22/23
WNYC	Illustration: composers		2000	99
Gene Wolsk	Ad: *Mastergate*		1989	126
Women in Advertising	Cover: *Information Highway*		1990	115
Yabadoo Productions	Poster: *Trophies*		1996	29

Notes:
I couldn't have created the digital files necessary for the production of this book all by myself.
I had a lot of help from Noah Hilsenrad, a design student at Parsons; Christine Cirker, a computer
maven and my son, Jack, who was in the seventh grade at the time. I am grateful for the support
and inspired scrutiny of Sara, my wife, and the people at Graphis: B.Martin Pedersen, Doug Wolske,
Andrea Birnbaum, Michael Gerbino, Lauren Slutsky and Joe Liotta.

For bean counters: number of jobs by decades: 50s: 9, 60s: 17, 70s: 19, 80s: 24, 90s: 45
since '00: 16.

Jobs rejected by the client are indicated by*

When I end things
I wish they were only beginning.